FOR THE LOVE OF CHARLIE

ROY JOHNSON

FOR THE LOVE OF CHARLIE

ROY JOHNSON

All rights reserved. No part of this publication may be reproduced, stored in any retrieval system or transmitted in any form or by any means, electronic, mechanical, photocopying, recording or otherwise, without the prior written permission of the copyright holder for which application should be addressed in the first instance to the publishers. The views expressed herein are those of the author and do not necessarily reflect the opinion or policy of Tricorn Books or the employing organisation, unless specifically stated. No liability shall be attached to the author, the copyright holder or the publishers for loss or damage of any nature suffered as a result of the reliance on the reproduction of any of the contents of this publication or any errors or omissions in the contents.

ISBN 978-1-914615-14-6

A CIP catalogue record for this book
is available from the British Library

Published 2021 Tricorn Books
Aspex Portsmouth
42 The Vulcan Building
Gunwharf Quays
Portsmouth PO1 3BF
Printed & bound in the UK

FOR THE LOVE OF CHARLIE

Contents

FOR THE LOVE OF CHARLIE

The Author

Roy Johnson was born in Malden Road Wymering, Portsmouth, Hampshire on 14th of October 1948. He had various jobs during his life, and he retired four years early due to a neck injury.

His last employment was as a cleansing technician with a local council and he retired in September 2009. He has been married to his wife Teresa since 1989. He is the youngest of four siblings and the only boy. His hobbies are fishing, both sea and game. He is also a military re-enactor with the Fort Cumberland Guard of Portsmouth. They recreate the history of the Royal Marines of the 1830s to 1860s.

Roy is also a stand-up comic and has entertained for charity concerts and shows for many years. His biggest moment to date came in December 1992 when he appeared on Noel's House Party. Roy is also a confirmed Christian and his favourite charity is animal welfare.

Chapter One
The Early Years

On my retirement in 2009, my wife and I decided to love and own a dog again. We had been unable to own one for the past ten years, due to our work commitments, but it had now become possible due to my retirement. So both my wife and I agreed to having a dog again. So we started our search for a dog, but our search didn't take long, for we found a **pets for sale** column in one of the newspapers. We found an ad which read

Labrador Greyhound Cross for sale, black with white patch, aged about two. £120. Telephone Poole.

So we phoned and a lady answered. She told us that the dog was still up for sale. So we then agreed to come to see the dog and it was arranged for us to see it the next day.

My wife and I at the time were living on a housing estate near to Portsmouth called Wecock. So we drove to Poole. The journey took us approximately an hour. On arrival, the area looked quite nice. It was kind of middle class. We found the dog owner's house and we knocked on the door. We were expecting to hear the dog to bark. But no, there was complete silence. So we knocked again and still no sound of a dog. So we knocked once more and the lady answered.

We said, "We never heard the dog bark."

"No, he don't bark," she said. "It's a very quiet dog."

I thought it a bit odd for most dogs bark when people knock on a door. I then said, "No worries. Can we see the dog?"

"Yes," she said. "But can you go around the back garden, please? And I'll bring him out to you."

I thought people would normally invite you in; I felt like a tradesperson back in Victorian England. I suppose it takes all sorts.

So there we were, waiting in the back garden to see the dog. Shortly after, she came out with the dog and the sight before our eyes was pitiful. Its head and body was almost skeletal in appearance, with its ribs protruding. The poor thing was a sorrowful sight, it was obvious to us the animal had been left starved and neglected. My wife and I were stunned at what we were witnessing before our eyes.

I felt anger towards this woman but withheld it inside. For I felt if I should show this, then she may ask us to leave and this would leave the poor animal to a terrible fate. So I held my true feelings back. By now I had decided to have this poor animal, so I could give it love and a happier life. But not just yet for I wanted to fathom out how this poor dog had ended up in an awful condition. So I had to be tactful with my questions, for I did not want to be shown the door and leave this dog behind.

My first question was, "He appears to be a little thinner than most dogs of his breed?"

"Oh!" she said, "that's just its breed."

My next question was, "What do you feed him on?"

She said, "Oh you know, the usual scraps etc."

I then asked, "Has he been inoculated against any canine diseases?"

"Oh yes," she said, "but we lost his records."

I then asked, 'Do you have the address of the vet? He may have records of his vaccines on their files."

"Oh!" she said. "To be honest, we forgot which vet we took him to."

My final question was, "What's his name?"

"Oh," she said, "we call him Chalky."

After the questions I had asked, it was obvious to me that what she said was a pack of lies and she was covering up the truth and that this poor dog had been starved and neglected. Her only interest in this animal was to get some money.

My wife Teresa had not said a word. I do believe she was in utter shock at the whole situation. Both my wife and I looked down and we were stroking Chalky. He lifted his head and was looking up at us. He had such wonderful big brown eyes. He was so appealing and full of love. I felt a sense of him saying, 'please take me away from here. Please help me.'

And at that moment, I said to my wife,

"Shall we have him?"

"Oh, yes, please," she said.

I knew she would say yes. But I had to ask, for it wasn't fair on her for me to make the decision for her. So I handed out the £120 and Chalky was now ours.

He was now family and we were now his adopted mum and dad. Chalky was now in our car on his way to his new home and new life with us; a life which will be filled with love and respect for him. On our journey back we stopped at a shopping mall and got some tinned food, biscuits and some treats for Chalky. I got back into the car and offered him a handful of doggy biscuits. He just lunged into my hands, scoffing all the treats with a great force, almost taking my hand off. We could see he was desperate for food.

I gave him several more handfuls of biscuits and also a couple of doggy chews. The look on Chalky's face was a picture;

for once in his life someone had shown him some love and affection. For this was another thing that he had been deprived of, but not anymore. His life was about to change for the better. We're about to fill it with love, happiness and joy.

We had decided to change his name from Chalky to Charlie, for Charlie was my late father's name and also my middle name. After a couple of months, Charlie was looking more like a healthy dog should look like. His life had changed for the better.

But on occasions he would show signs of his cruelly treated past. On one occasion I was taking my belt off in front of him and he started shaking and shivering and then just ran into another room. I realised he must have been beaten in the past. There was also another sign of his past, he would never set foot in the kitchen. Even if we put his favourite treats just inside the kitchen. He would never venture inside to retrieve them. I knew the kitchen held cruel memories from his past. We often wondered why he was so afraid to enter. I had a feeling with his previous owners, him being so hungry through neglect, he would smell food and probably tried to find the food by going into the kitchen. Then when the owners found him, they most probably had beaten him and now he feels he may be beaten again.

But of course, this is just speculation.

All Teresa and I wanted is to let Charlie somehow realise that he is safe and that Teresa and I would never hurt Charlie in any way whatsoever. If only he could realise this for we love him very much.

***

Chapter Two
The Middle Years

Charlie was now five years old and had become a valued member of our family.

He had become quite clever. He had learned the words of places where I took him on his walks. Most dogs know the word 'walkies' and Charlie did too, but he also knew named places where I used to walk him as well. For instance, if I said 'up the woods, want to go woods?' he would know what I meant. A walk in the woods, or I would simply say 'seaside, want to go seaside?' Then he knew he was going for a walk on the beach. His favourite local walk was Portsdown Hill, which looks over the city of Portsmouth. It's a firm favourite with all dog walkers. All I need say for that is 'up the hill'. Then there's the park, just saying 'park' and he knew he'd be going to the park.

But if I had no plans for taking him out, and he wanted to go, then he would sit up, right in front of me and give me a big stare with those big brown loving eyes of his and sometimes he would give a little whimper as well, so that I would take notice of him and then in the end I would just give in to him. He would wait for my usual routine which would be a stretch out with my arms and I would say I suppose so. He would then go bonkers, get his way and he would have his walk.

Another favourite word he liked to hear was 'motorcar', simply that. If I said motorcar, it would mean he was going on a mystery walk somewhere unknown. And Charlie used to love being out in the car.

We were living on the second floor of a two-storey block of flats on a housing estate, known as the Wecock estate, which is about ten miles from Portsmouth.

Behind our accommodation was a park and woodland. So it was ideal for walking Charlie. However, a ground-floor flat in that regard would be more suitable for Charlie.

In our present accommodation, we have to go down two flights of stairs; if we had a garden we could on nice days leave the door open and then Charlie could go in and out of the garden of his own free will.

So my wife Teresa and I thought it was a good idea. So we went to the council next day and put our names down on the housing transfer list.

It was now a case of just wait and see.

It was a lovely sunny June day. Charlie was sat in his bed. I looked at him and said, "Up the park?"

That's all it took. He jumped out of his bed and was very excited. So we headed for the park. There were other dogs there with other owners and Charlie joined in the fun with the other dogs.

They were running around in circles and chasing balls. They were loving it in the June sunshine. Then from nowhere a cat crossed Charlie's path so Charlie gave chase and ran out of sight through some hedges.

I was panicking. I did not know which way to turn and was worried.

A good hour had now passed and still no sight or sound of Charlie. Some friendly dog walkers had seen what had happened and they offered to help in my search and to hunt for Charlie.

Time was ticking and still no sign of Charlie. By now I was getting very worried and anxious. And to make things worse, I could hear the sound of a car's screeching brakes.

My thoughts then turned to horror. I

was thinking the worst has happened; there were some of the other walkers who asked if they could help by keeping their eyes peeled for Charlie while I took the car out to search around the Wecock Estate

My mind was running riot as I drove around searching each road I turned into. I had thoughts and fears of maybe seeing him lying injured or, worse still, finding him dead.

These thoughts would do me no good.

I had to be focused. By now I'd covered a fair area so decided to return to the park.

Then total and utter relief, one of the dog walkers had found Charlie and was holding him by the collar.

I could not thank him enough and I offered him a reward. He said no, not at all. He said it was nothing. "Charlie had found them and had just trotted back through the park, probably looking for you," he said, Well, I gave Charlie a big hug and said, "Don't do that to me again, Charlie."

A year had passed and then one morning a letter came through the postbox from the council housing department. It was good news. The ground-floor flat with a garden had come up for offer. It was located at a place called Crookhorn, which was about three or four miles away from our present address. It was a nice clean pleasant area, located near to a park and a woodland. Also a short distance away was Portsdown Hill with its fantastic views looking over Portsmouth with the Isle of Wight further in the distance.

There are also four forts along this hill, Fort Purbrook, Fort Widley, Fort Southwick and Fort Nelson. They were built in the 19th century by Lord Palmerston. They were built in case of attack from the French but no attack ever took place, because Napoleon was being beaten on the battlefield at Waterloo, which ended on Sunday, June 18th 1815. After that, the forts were known as Palmerston's Follies.

Also in the area of Crookhorn is a precinct of shops – just a small precinct but adequate for our needs. There is also a church opposite the precinct and a pub nearby to socialise in and if we fell ill then a doctors surgery was close by as well. As the only accommodation on offer, we found it quite nice.

It was a house separated into two flats, one up and one down. There was a front and rear garden to the ground-floor flat which was the one that was offered to us.

Inside was a small kitchen leading from the hallway. And also opposite the kitchen was a shower room and toilet. Then at the end of the hall was the lounge and adjacent to that was the bedroom.

The flat was ideal for us, with the added bonus of a garden for Charlie to play in and for him to watch out from. So it was decided upon and we accepted the council's offer and moved in a few days later.

Also in the area was a college and so students would walk through this estate to reach the college. At the time, my wife and I thought that may be a problem as being in large groups, there could be some small numbers of students that could cause trouble. But no! We found all the students that passed through the estate were all well behaved and also very polite. So we moved into the estate in February 2014.

Charlie was now around six years old. He loved his new-found garden and would spend hours just sitting out there. When he was out there we always made sure the front door was open for him. And we could see him from our front hallway. This gave him the freedom to go in and out of our flat as and when he wanted to. Each day he would sit in the garden just watching the students passing and also getting to know our local neighbours as they passed his gate. Some of our neighbours also had dogs, which Charlie had got to know. They would have conversations with each other, they would yell and bark at each other in their doggy fashion. And while this commotion went on, it made for a good opportunity to get to know their owners. And over time this proved to form friendships with our neighbours and those who passed by Charlie's gate. Some would give Charlie treats at the gate, then eventually, as he got to know them and if he saw them approaching the gate, he would bark at them so they would take notice of him. And if he was lucky they would pass him some treats. This became a regular habit between the neighbours and Charlie.

My wife and I had fitted in well with our neighbours in the neighbourhood and had made some good friends. Charlie loved being in his garden. It was only a small garden but he loved it. And the neighbours loved to see him sitting in it. He didn't always get treats, some passers-by who came up to his gate just stroked and made a fuss of him.

Charlie also got on well with the neighbourhood dogs. They would stop at his gate with their owners and start barking out to each other on either side of the gate. The neighbour above us whose name was Colin would often throw down treats to Charlie from his flat above, that looked down into Charlie's garden. Charlie had got used to this, and grew to expect it. Charlie had a regular routine. Every time he walked out into his garden he would look up at Colin's window and if Colin wasn't there, he would bark out for him so that he got his daily treat.

Colin told me Charlie was the best dog in the world. This brought a lump to my throat knowing our neighbour Colin felt that way about him.

To the left of us was a large block of flats. There were three dogs there and their owners and we got to know them for their visits to **Charlie's Gate**.

It become a focal point to meet up and have a daily chin-wag and of course Charlie's doggy friends enjoyed meeting up too. There was Kevin and Tracy with their dog Lily, then followed by Melanie with her dog Pooh; then a couple of blocks down from us was June with her two King

Charles spaniels; and two blocks from her was Margaret with her Jack Russell, Millie, who was constantly barking at everything, especially when she met up with Charlie – there would be one hell of a telling off between them. The whole neighbourhood knew of those two when they met up. Our neighbours Kevin and Tracey always brought Charlie a treat, but on one occasion they forgot to bring out his treat and just walked past his gate and they were hoping he wouldn't notice, but no such luck. He was having none of it. He howled at them as they passed, he just would not stop until he got his way.

And by now Kevin and Tracy were in fits of laughter. So they walked back to **Charlie's Gate** and Kevin stayed there while Tracy walked up three flights of stairs just to get Charlie his daily treat from them.

She said, "The things we have to do to

Charlie aged about five

Charlie relaxing at home

Charlie and his pal Jed, who passed on

Photo of the authors sisters dog Sacha - who passed on

Charlie with his owner, the author

A view of Charlies garden

keep the peace with Charlie."

So now Charlie was happy knowing he had not been forgotten by Kevin and Tracy and it was now permitted for them to continue on with their day.

Charlie knew that not all who passed his gate gave out treats. But those who did offer them, they were marked and he would never forget their face. From that moment on he would expect more treats every time he saw you pass by his gate. He got to know those who gave treats from those who did not, for some neighbours were busy going off to work, like Chris who lived in the block of flats to our left. Chris would always stop for a quick hello, to give Charlie a quick cuddle before going on his way but even a sign of affection such as that Charlie would remember, but if he saw that person again he would give them a look as if to say, 'don't forget my daily cuddle before you go to work.'

And Charlie will always be looking out for him both in the morning and night. Charlie's only aim in life was getting treats, going for walks and playing with his toys. He had become much loved by Teresa and I and was also shown love from our friends and neighbours. Charlie had come from a hell of an existence and from being unloved and unwanted to then to become loved and to be much wanted. He was now having a life worth living, a life filled with love. He was a soft-hearted soul and when he looked into your eyes with those big brown eyes of his, you would feel your heart melt for him and just had to give him a big loving hug.

Charlie was becoming more and more popular in the area. Even the postman bringing our mail would say hello to Charlie, for Charlie would probably be sitting by or just inside of our front door.

Neighbours Danny and Sue who lived next door to the right of us have a large white cat called Barney, and Barney the cat is a real character. He would come to **Charlie's Gate** and sit and stare through the wooden slats of the gate.

Charlie would go mad when he saw Barney boldly sitting there. He would run around in circles then look at Barney through the gateposts, just sitting there staring at him. Barney would then turn his back on Charlie then would kind of shrug his shoulders and just walk on his way, as if to say, 'Oh, what the hell, stupid dog.' It was amusing to watch and it became a regular occurrence with both Charlie and Barney.

Chapter Three
The Later Years

There was this one day and the birds were singing, the sky was blue. It was truly a lovely, wonderful day and I just looked at Charlie and said, "Up the hill, want to go up the hill?" He knew what I meant.

Portsdown Hill, which is about a five-minute drive away and was Charlie's favourite local walk. So I drove to the hill which had lots of rabbits. The best times to see them was early morning and late afternoon. It was now around midday when I took Charlie for a run; there was still a chance of seeing the odd rabbit, Charlie just loved to chase rabbits.

So there we were, Charlie and me on Portsdown Hill. I let Charlie off his lead and he ran down the hill and was foraging around, trying to find a rabbit to chase. I was following behind, watching him enjoy himself, he was truly loving it. Then he saw a rabbit, which he started to stalk; then the rabbit sensed that Charlie was close by, so took off at speed. Charlie was close behind, he chased the rabbit which ran into a convenient hedge and unfortunately disappeared.

Then Charlie and I continued further down the hill until we eventually reached the bottom, the steepness of the hill towered above us. It was easy to go down the hill but walking back up was tough going. When walking back up, I would walk then stop for a while, then continue on and so on. When I was younger, I could just walk up all the way without stopping and think nothing of it. But at this moment in time I was in my late 60s and Charlie was around five or six, and still had bags of energy.

We were enjoying this gorgeous sunny July day with the wildflowers looking splendid in the bright sunshine, and then Charlie spotted a rabbit and gave chase. The rabbit was running and zig-zagging as Charlie chased him. Then the rabbit ran into a large bush with Charlie in hot pursuit. Then I heard a loud crying *Yelp*, followed by a whimper. Charlie had somehow hurt himself inside that bush. The bush was very dense and I could not see him but I could hear him crying and whimpering. Then I heard him again but the sound was behind me now. So I looked around and there he was, he must have come through the bush either from the back or from the side and then ended up behind me. I noticed that he was limping badly and could hardly walk so I knelt down to him and then saw blood pouring from his top inside leg.

He needed urgent treatment or he

could bleed to death. My problem now was I had to get to the top of the steep hill to where the car was parked and then I had to drive him to the nearest vet, which was about another three miles from there.

So there I was with Charlie with blood pouring from his wound.

I felt helpless because I had nothing to use to stop the blood from pouring out.

All I could think of was, I must get him to a vet quickly, very quickly. But my biggest problem was to get him up this hill to the car.

It was tiring at the best of times, but now I had the added task of carrying Charlie in my arms as well. But it had to be done, otherwise Charlie could die of loss of blood.

I was now pushing myself as quickly as I could. I felt exhausted and feeling breathless as I pushed myself forward. I did my very best to keep going, but I was no spring chicken.

I was praying for strength to keep going; every step I took was a step closer to saving Charlie. The clock was ticking, every second counted as I forced myself forward. The peak of the hill was upon me. I was there at last. By now I was gasping for breath, and my legs were aching as well as my arms after I'd been carrying him up that steep hill.

I was now in my car on my way to the vets. My shirt was soaked in blood from Charlie's wound. Charlie was on the passenger seat of the car and was looking weak. This added more worrying thoughts. Like will I make it on time to save him. All these thoughts were going through my mind as I drove on to the vets.

Then my mobile phone rang, but I let it ring for I was driving. Then it dawned on me, I had not yet phoned my wife Teresa. But come to think of it, I didn't have time to phone out with the situation I was in.

Finally I reached the vet and he was rushed in for treatment straightaway.

The vet told me to go home and he would phone me when he'd finished working on Charlie.

So I phoned Teresa to give her the news about Charlie.

She got emotional over the phone. I told her not to worry for I was sure he would be okay now he was with the vet.

I then told her I was on my way home. Then on arrival back home I gave Teresa a hug and told her not to worry. It was now a matter of waiting for the phone call from the vet.

About three hours had passed and we were waiting and then the phone rang. It was the call we were counting on, in the hope that Charlie was okay. The vet said it was good news. Charlie's okay. They managed to stop the bleeding and the wounds were now stitched up. He said it was close. If there had been more blood loss, then it would have been fatal. But thankfully that wasn't the case.

Charlie was now safe and back home. I reported the bush where Charlie hurt himself to the council, as other dogs could get hurt. The council checked it out and they found tangled inside the bush was a large amount of barbed wire. They removed the whole bush and the barbed wire. I felt good after its removal; no more dogs would come to harm.

My nephew Vincent used to visit us with his dog Jed. Charlie loved Jed and Vincent's visits. When he arrived, Charlie and Jed would play and have fun together. They became buddies. And it was nice seeing them have fun together.

When Vince was coming, and he was bringing Jed, I'd just say to Charlie, "Jed is coming" and then Charlie would go berserk with excitement.

It was great seeing Jed and Charlie together and there were times when we took both dogs on walks in the woods etc. Jed was a chocolate coloured labrador. Also Jed was a big softy with a big loving heart, just like Charlie, and both dogs were great pals together.

And one day Vincent phoned me said he'd got some sad news. Jed had become ill and the vet said he had cancer and there was nothing they could do for him and he was put to sleep.

After Jed's death, Vincent came to visit and Charlie got excited and was looking around for Jed. He ran out into the garden and looked up the road for him and he could not understand why

Jed was not with Vincent. For when he saw Vincent, Jed always came along. Charlie became very sad, he could not understand where Jed had gone, all we could do was give Charlie lots of cuddles. What else could we do but give Charlie lots and lots of love?

I also gave Charlie extra walks and play times in the hope I would take his mind off Jed's loss. I asked my nephew Vincent to visit less often because each time he saw Vincent he thought maybe Jed was close by. I still saw Vincent but I would visit him at his house instead.

My sister Brenda had a delightful little dog called Sasha and both her and Charlie got on well together. They would run around together in my sister's garden. My sister's house is in Emsworth, Hampshire, and there is a very nice harbour and shoreline. My sister and I used to walk Sasha and Charlie together on harbour walks. Charlie loved charging into the sea chasing after balls. A few months had passed since our last walk and Sasha had now become ill. She had an examination at the vets, and it was not good news. The test showed that she had bowel cancer and the vet informed my sister that the best thing they could do for Sasha was for her to be put to sleep. My sister agreed.

Brenda was devastated even though Sasha lived to a good age. She was 16. It was hard for my sister for she had also lost her husband a few years earlier. She was now living alone, but she did have three grown-up sons that came to visit. Also my wife and I paid her visits as well. And now our Charlie had lost another of his little pals. So more hugs for Charlie, plus more walks and playtime to take his mind off.

Two pets in our family circle had now

passed on and we needed a distraction to cheer ourselves up a little. We had a good friend of ours, who lived in Mitchelstown, County Cork, Ireland, and we would stay at his place for a couple of weeks. And Charlie could come as well. My friend was David O'Connell, a long-standing friend who used to live in England and moved to Ireland in 1981.

We took the Pembroke to Rosslare ferry. Charlie hated the ferry crossing. He had to be in a cage below decks and he was whining.

He didn't like to be in the cage. The ferry crossing took four hours. I felt sorry for Charlie in that cage, he was out of his comfort zone. He was glad to be back on dry land.

My friend Dave was retired like me, he had served for many years as a post office area manager. So here we were on a holiday in the Emerald Isle of Ireland.

The land of the 40 shades of green.

We were enjoying the views of the lakes of Killarney and the Ring of Kerry, the Torc Waterfall and the Gap of Dunloe, the magnificent Cliffs of Moher and on to Blarney Castle to kiss the Blarney Stone. Then we stopped at lovely beaches like the Inch Strand.

We then went on to Dingle to see Fungi the dolphin. Charlie was loving it and was having a good time on all the lovely beaches, then one beach we stopped at there were lots of old trawler wrecks among the sand dunes. The tide was out and the beach consisted of a mixture of sand and mud and was quite desolate.

We weren't sure of the name of the beach for we had only stopped to stretch our legs, after our long drive. Charlie was enjoying himself foraging around the sand dunes. He then walked onto the beach when suddenly a large seagull flew out in front of him and was flying out to sea at a low level. And Charlie being Charlie gave chase after the large gull. The gull kept going and so did Charlie. He thought it was great fun, but there was a danger ahead in the form of soft mud. I called out to him to come back but he was more interested in the gull and just kept going, heading into danger. Dave said there's danger out there you could lose him in the soft mud and the further he goes the higher the danger. I was panicking and moved towards Charlie. I'd only gone a few yards and Dave grabbed me from behind and said, "Do not go, this is a dangerous area. The mud will swallow you up."

So those words made me even more worried and concerned about Charlie. All we could do was to call out to him and pray to God to save him. By now we were yelling and screaming to Charlie to come back. He was so far away. I was wondering if he could actually hear us calling for it was a long way out and I could see that the mud was up to his chest. Then we saw his hindquarters sink down, which left his front legs on top of the mud. It was as if he sat down into the mud so he could lift his front half up. By now, I, Teresa and our friend Dave, were getting really concerned for Charlie from where we were watching. It appeared Charlie was fighting a losing battle.

We could see him struggling to pull himself out; we were by now getting emotional. I was very, very worried. I started praying to God for help – please, please God help our wonderful dog Charlie. We love him so very, very much. Please help him. Please don't let him die. Then at that very moment, I felt my prayer had been answered. Charlie had suddenly found a foothold and was pulling himself up and was heaving himself out from the mud.

We were calling to 'Come on Charlie, come on' and then total relief. He managed it and was now running back to us. And then thank God, Charlie was safe and back with us. He was panting heavily. We gave him a big hug and said, "Thank you, God. Thank you very much for saving our wonderful dog, Charlie." I'm sure that God was on Charlie's side that day.

So after that, we picked ourselves up and got on with the rest of our holiday with the knowledge that our Charlie was now safe after that awful experience. It was a nightmare of an ordeal that we had gone through on that day, and one that we would not want to experience again.

But life goes on and so did our holiday in Ireland. We did a lot of touring thanks to our friend Dave, for he knew the area well and took us to all the best areas in and around Ireland.

While there in Ireland, we also got to know the locals and friends of Dave's that lived and worked in Mitchelstown, County Cork.

In fact, we got to know them very well and went out to the local bars for nights out with them. And believe me, there's no atmosphere like the atmosphere that you get from a real Irish pub.

The Irish are a really friendly bunch and will make any stranger feel welcome. So our holiday had come to an end, a holiday that we shall remember in more ways than one.

***

A year had now passed and Teresa and I had booked another holiday. This time we put ourselves on a Med cruise. I had a good friend whose name is Ricky Poulton. And Ricky was going to look after Charlie while we were away on the cruise. Charlie knew Ricky as he used to visit and we've gone on walks with Charlie with him.

So Teresa and I would be going on our cruise with the peace of mind that Charlie would be safe in the care of Ricky.

But we would be bound to miss him.

We would hate to leave him but we knew he would be in good hands with Ricky.

And so the cruise date arrived and all our packing was done and we were ready for the off but first to take Charlie to Ricky. On arrival at Ricky's, Charlie was excited to see him. He had always enjoyed Ricky's company from his past visits, but I felt that Charlie was expecting to return home after his visit, just like he had always done, but not on this occasion.

The time had come for me to say goodbye to Charlie. So I then looked at Charlie and said, "Got to go now. And we'll see you later. Ricky will look after you, love you." Charlie gave me a stare as I went to wave goodbye to him. I could only describe the look on his face as pitiful. As I was making my way out of Ricky's, the look I was getting made me feel so guilty. So I just had to go back and give him one final hug.

I said, "Sorry, sweetheart. I've got to go now, got to go, you'll be okay with Ricky. See you soon, love you."

So then I had to force myself away. I had to make our way to the cruise port in Southampton.

So anyway, our Med cruise went ahead and we had a fabulous time. The entertainment, the food and hospitality was all first class.

But there was just one drawback. We missed Charlie. There wasn't a day went by when we didn't wonder about him. We knew he was safe at Ricky's, but we could not help thinking of him. He was probably wondering where we were and was probably missing his garden and his daily routine, seeing and greeting the dogs and neighbours who passed his gate on a daily basis and of course his daily treats, especially those from Colin who lived in the flat above us.

***

So we were now back in Southampton docks, and we just had to disembark from the cruise liner which had been our home for the past 12 days. The first thing to do was to phone Ricky to say we're back and on our way to collect Charlie.

He said, "Charlie's been fine. I've made a lot of fuss of him since you've been gone. Charlie has shown signs of missing you both, like sitting by the front door looking out for your return home."

I said, "Don't worry. You can tell Charlie, mummy and daddy are on their way home."

And so we were on our way to collect our Charlie and when we arrived at Ricky's we knocked on the door. Charlie could be heard on the other side of the door. He was barking out loud and was getting very excited. He knew it was us outside trying to get in. There was no response from Ricky so we knocked a third time. Then a voice called out saying, "I'm not in." He had just arrived back. "I went to the local shop for some bread and milk." He then said, "He's been 12 days without you, I'm sure you can wait a second or two longer. Wait while I find my door key." So Ricky located his key and opened the front door.

Charlie then went wild with excitement. His tail was whizzing round, he was jumping up on us and was growling with excitement. I then said, "Ricky, it's no good, I can't stay a moment longer. I need to get Charlie home for he is overexcited."

And I expected Charlie had missed his garden and his friends that walk by and say hello to him. So I thanked Ricky for looking after Charlie for us and then paid him for his care and time looking after him.

As we arrived home, Colin was there to greet Charlie and threw Charlie a treat which is a daily routine that Charlie had missed for the last fortnight.

Then shortly after, Kevin and Tracy

came around with their dog Lily. This was followed by Anne and her dog Lulu, then Margaret with her dog Millie, then followed Melanie and her little dog Pooh.

All of Charlie's friends were now here to welcome Charlie home. Then later in the day, Chris came round to also welcome Charlie back home. Chris was not a dog owner but he always made a fuss of Charlie and today was no exception. He gave Charlie a big hug and said, "Welcome home, Charlie," but it wasn't all about Charlie and he also said it was nice to see us back and we were all glad we had a nice holiday. So there we were back home and back to normal. The cruise was great. It was also great to be back home. For as the saying goes, there's no place like home.

***

Another year had now passed and we were thinking about having another holiday. Teresa and I love going on holidays but the thought of leaving Charlie alone again was a difficult one, and was holding us back.

Then on one occasion Teresa and I went out for the day with Charlie and we were on the beach at Hayling Island.

Charlie was loving it, running along the beach and going into the sea as we threw his ball for him.

Charlie always loved going into the water – any water, be it a river, pond, sea or lake, he just loved frolicking around in it.

Water was like a magnet to him. He couldn't get enough of it. Anyway, a day on Hayling beach had come to an end and we were on our way back home. While on our journey I spotted a car sales forecourt and I noticed a camper van on it that was up for sale.

"That's it," I said. "A camper van, we could get a camper van. We could go all over in it. And guess what? Charlie could come along as well." We could share our holidays together, myself, Teresa and Charlie. Teresa told me she agreed with the idea. So the next day we went out in search of a camper van. We found a dealership solely selling camper vans. There are plenty to choose from. They came in all sorts of sizes and conditions. There was one that took her eye, for it wasn't too small or too large. It was somewhere in the middle. It was okay to fit in the parking bay without causing a problem, provided there was no height barriers. The camper we liked was a two-berth but had room enough for Charlie's bed. There was plenty of cupboard space plus a cooker, fridge, sink unit and a toilet. It also had two bays which could also be used as seats once the large cushions were put into place. It also had a table for two. It was ideal for a couple like ourselves, but not for a family. It was just right for what we wanted, and it was also in our price range. So we were happy with this campervan. Teresa was happy, I was happy, so we went ahead and made the purchase. Then shortly after that, we also sold our car for we found we had no need for two vehicles as it meant twice the insurance and twice the cost of road tax, etc.

The camper would cover all our needs, it could fit into a car parking space which meant it was easy to park at say a supermarket to do our shopping etc. The only place that we could not park in was a car park with a height restriction barrier.

So we were all set to go on holiday. Good news that Charlie could come too.

So we decided to take the camper van to the Lake District which was around an eight-hour journey.

As it was such a long drive we decided to make a stopover halfway. So this we did and then after a good night's sleep in the camper, we continued with our journey on the following day, heading for the Lake District.

Then on arrival we found a very nice touring park right alongside Lake Windermere, which is just a couple of miles from Bowness, which is a pretty little lakeside town and if you wish you could go on a boat trip on Lake Windermere. There were plenty of walks in the area too, which was great news for our Charlie, also for me. I brought my fly rod along so I could occupy myself with a bit of fly fishing.

And I'd been told that there was a chance of a trout or even a char if I was lucky. I've caught lots of fish during my lifetime but the Lake District I had nothing, not a touch; but fishing is not about just catching fish. It's about trying, taking in what's all around you. Hearing the birds singing and the bees buzzing, and Charlie barking for me to show attention towards him And of course, how can you possibly forget him? And so my fishing had to cease, so I could pay attention to Charlie and take him for a walk through the lovely surroundings of Lake Windermere.

During our holiday, we also found a steam railway with spectacular scenic views. Charlie loved it on that steam train ride, especially the attention he was getting from the other passengers. With remarks like 'Isn't he lovely?' 'Can I stroke him?' 'Can I hug him?'

Charlie taking it all in and enjoying all the attention. Charlie was also enjoying the views from the window.

He was like this with any vehicles, he just loved to sit and look out of the windows when he is on the move.

We had a lovely holiday in the Lake District and it never ended there. We had holidays in Wales, Devon, Dorset, Somerset, Cornwall, Yorkshire, the east coast of England, Norfolk Broads, Skegness, Scarborough, York the Midlands.

And the list went on and on.

Our camper van was our holiday accommodation. We went to lots of interesting places with Charlie enjoying it.

It was now coming into winter so we eased up on trips with the camper and decided for spring to arrive before deciding on any more breaks away.

When spring did arrive, we took a week away in Weymouth. We had been to Weymouth many times before and always enjoyed the fun times there. The beach was lovely and Sandy and Charlie loved it. They're running in the sea and chasing and playing with other dogs etc.

We were now back home after our break in Weymouth. It was 2018 and Charlie was around ten years old and showing signs of greyness around his snout and bits of grey around his eyes and ears. But for a ten-year-old he had a fair bit of energy, especially if he saw a squirrel or a rabbit to chase after. On one particular sunny afternoon, I took him on one of his favourite walks up on Portsdown Hill, but this time higher up. Below was a busy road that ran the full length of the hill. It ran from Bedhampton, which is near the town of Havant, and went for about 12 miles to Fareham, which is another town in Hampshire.

So here we were, Charlie and me. I put

him on his lead because of the busy road about 100 yards below me. And then out of the blue, a loud bang rang out, which was most likely a shotgun and probably someone shooting rabbits. But the worst thing was, as soon as the shot rang out, Charlie ran off at speed and pulled his lead clean out of my hand. And worse was to come. Charlie had run into the busy road below; cars and a large van screeched to a halt. My heart was in my mouth, with my hands covering my face. I felt panicked and was extremely worried.

I ran at speed down the hill. Charlie was just sat there on this busy road with the traffic brought to a halt. And a large van was just inches away from him. I gave the driver of the van a wave and said, "Thank you so very much." He said, "As long as he is okay, that's fine with me." I picked up Charlie and got him off the road.

All I wanted to do then was to get home and relax and just calm down. Once home, I told Teresa what had happened. She said, "Oh no, not again. They say things like this come in threes." And in Charlie's case that was true. Firstly, he nearly bled to death after cutting himself on barbed wire on Portsdown Hill. On holiday in Ireland he nearly met his fate on the beach with very soft sand and mud and got caught out and nearly got swallowed and dragged under the soft mud. And now was almost run over and killed on Portsdown Hill road.

I think God was on his side again today. Charlie's our world. We nearly lost him again. And the angel shined on him again today.

Chapter Four
The Twilight Years

A year had passed. It was now 2019. Charlie was around 11 years old now. That's getting to be elderly in dog years, he was also a little slower and like any OAP, he was showing more greyish fur. Our love for Charlie had grown stronger and stronger and Charlie was now in his twilight years of life. Over the years, we've had Charlie, he has given us unconditional love, he has brought sunshine into our lives. And he has given us joy and happiness and has filled our hearts with love. He was getting slower these days. When I took him out he played less energetically. He used to love going along Portsdown Hill, but nowadays he would walk just a few yards then pull back and want to return to the camper van to go back home.

***

Another year had passed. It was now the year 2020, in the month of September.

And there have been many restrictions owing to the Coronavirus pandemic, but the government had lifted restrictions on camping and touring camps and caravan sites and we were given the green light, so to speak. So we decided to get away for a week's break and head to Ilfracombe in North Devon. We found a nice camper touring park there with plenty of amenities, including onsite walking areas for dogs. But Charlie just wanted to sit or lay around and showed little interest if I threw a ball. He would just do nothing. I began to worry now for Charlie, and when we returned home I tried to take him for a small local walk and would just walk outside the gate then he'd pull back and just wanted to go back indoors.

***

Five months had passed. It was now February 2021.

Charlie was aged around 12. Although he had slowed up, he didn't appear to be ill in any way. But by mid February he started to go off his food; he even left his biscuits and stopped taking treats from our neighbours.

Then I said to Teresa, "There's something wrong with Charlie. I think we should get him checked out." We took him to our usual vets. It was 2nd March 2021.

Once we were at the vets they first checked for lumps over his body and found none, which was good news, for lumps are a sign it could be cancer. Then the vet said that his tummy doesn't feel right. And I said, "How come it doesn't feel right?"

The lady then said, "Well, his tummy feels solid and hard. It should be more soft and subtle to the touch." The vet told us she thought it best to give him a scan and see what's inside his tummy and other regions of his body. She then told us to go home and they would phone us later with the findings.

So Teresa and I returned home to wait for the call. Then after two or three hours we had the call from the vet they told us that there was no easy way of telling us, but the scan had shown there was a large tumour in Charlie's liver and a number of smaller tumours in other parts of his body. And also they had found he had internal bleeding and then said sorry but the best thing they could do for Charlie was to put him to sleep.

Our world at that moment fell apart. Teresa and I gave each other a hug. We both cried like babies. The thought about our wonderful Charlie no longer being here was unbearable and hard to take. We had to go back to the vets for our final goodbyes to Charlie.

On arriving at the vets, we were told that only one of us could be there while they carried out the procedure, due to the COVID restrictions at the time. Teresa asked that I be there while she waited outside. So it was agreed that it was me to be there, which was not going to be easy by any means.

When inside, there were two adjoining rooms: the first room was where I had to stay close by to Charlie and once I've done this, they would take Charlie to the adjoining room to carry out the procedure. And all I could do was watch from a distance by looking through from the other room.

The time had arrived and Charlie was brought in to me. He looked so sweet and loving, just as he always did. With those big brown eyes of his, he came up to me and wagged his tail. He was happy to see me and I felt at that moment he thought I'd come to take him back home. I then felt choked and tears filled my eyes. All I could do was cuddle him and say, "Mummy and daddy love you very very much. And we have come to say goodbye now for you're going to a new place now, a place where you can run with other doggies and you will be happy there and then one day mummy and daddy will go there too. And we will all be together again in heaven." But by now I could not speak, I was a mess.

Then the dreaded moment came and they took Charlie in the next room but not before I gave him one final big hug.

I watched from the next room as they put the needle in his right leg with his little face looking across to me with those big loving brown eyes of his and as they glazed over he just drifted away and he was gone. At that moment I felt my world had split apart but Charlie was so much more to us. He was a child we never had; he was our little boy. He was our baby.

And we brought him from a cruel existence to one of happiness and joy, a world we shared with him. Now he has gone from us, we feel a part of us has gone with him. He was very special and he had a heart that was full of love for us, now our hearts are full of love for him.

I met Teresa outside the vets. I was holding Charlie's collar and she came over to me and we both could not speak, we just hugged each other and our hearts were broken and we just fell apart. The vet put a pawprint of Charlie's on a card, plus a snip of his hair. We thanked her very much. It's a kind of wonderful thing she had done and we should treasure her gift to us. It was a part of Charlie and the gift will add to our memories of him.

Since Charlie's death, life has been hard without him. We doted on him. He was our little boy. He had brought love and happiness into our home. He gave us joy and he had become special to us. And I'm sure in that sweet little head of his we had become special to him, knowing how awful the first two years of his life were. I'm sure that God had looked down on him and brought us into his life to share his love with us and with it, we returned and shared our love with him. Charlie became a part of our family. He brought in extra joy and happiness to our home. He brought a warm feeling to our home and that warmth brought with it a bond between us – a family bond, because that's what we have become, a family. Charlie had put our life on a higher level, but sadly with the loss of our wonderful dog Charlie, our life has gone to a lower level.

***

We miss him so very much and it hurts, our home is not the same anymore. It's empty without him there.

There's a saying that goes home is not home without a dog in it. And for us, that's just how we feel now. Home is not our home without Charlie in it. They say that life goes on. That may be true, but for us, at present, it's just an existence, an empty existence.

A day later and the realisation that Charlie was no longer there was hard to take.

Home had become cold and empty without the warmth of Charlie's love to fill it.

That morning, I got up out of bed and walked into the kitchen to make a cup of coffee. Then I took a handful of biscuits from a plastic tub. Then walked into the hallway and put out Charlie's breakfast. The silence was deafening and then the realisation that Charlie was no longer there was heartbreaking.

My morning routine of getting out of bed and giving Charlie biscuits for his breakfast had been a regular habit for the last ten years. One that was not easily broken.

***

We had Charlie cremated at a pet crematorium and had arranged for his ashes to be returned to us and a few days later they had arrived by courier. Charlie's ashes were in a pine casket with a brass plaque on the top which simply read 'Charlie'.

Both Teresa and I hugged and cuddled Charlie's casket and we said, "You're home now, Charlie."

We buried these ashes in our back garden. And then we bought a cross with a brass plaque in the centre which read

Charlie RIP
always loved and never forgotten
2008 to 2021

We also had a brass plaque put on our front gate with inscription.

This garden was Charlie's garden, a wonderful dog, now at peace in God's garden.

The plaque was put there to keep Charlie's memory alive but it didn't end there. We also bought a dog statue from a garden centre that kind of resembles Charlie but I made a few alterations by painting a white patch on the chest. And then I also painted some grey tufts to his snout and other areas that made it look more like Charlie had looked in his later years. We didn't want it stolen so it would be put in our garden – sorry, *Charlie's Garden* – during the day when it would be brought in at night for safekeeping. Many of our neighbours who knew Charlie would comment on how realistic it looked and would say we thought it was like the real Charlie sitting there.

Then some would say you would think he was still sitting there looking at his garden waiting for his daily rations of treats from some of us neighbours. Just like he always did. Bless him. They said they were really missing him and seeing him come out to greet them each day. They said it was just not the same anymore without Charlie around, greeting them each day.

Their comments brought a lump to my throat. Just knowing how much he is missed around our neighbourhood and the love he shared with all known to him.

There was one final thing we did in his memory. We knew how much he enjoyed his holidays with us from going places in our camper. So we decided to name the camper after him. We both now call it Charlie and not only that. We've also put his name onto the camper as well. We placed his name at the rear on the top left side corner and also on both sides. We can now say when we go out that we are taking Charlie out for a run. A lot of love was shown by our neighbours and many of them also gave us sympathy cards on the loss of Charlie. We had lots of leftover pet food and biscuits after Charlie's death. And this we shared with our neighbours' pets. We felt Charlie would have wanted that; we also shared his toys with our neighbours' dogs.

But Charlie's collar needs to be kept ourselves so to remember him by his collar we put it onto Charlie's statue. We thought this was a fitting gesture to his memory and we also had a large canvas picture made of him, which we put on our lounge wall. It is also the books front cover.

We also have lots of memories of him on DVD discs. Charlie had, over time, from the first time we met him, changed our lives for the better. He brought us joy and happiness and most of all love. Charlie was more than just a dog. He was our baby. He was just a gentle soul, a big softy with a big heart. A heart filled with love. And now that he has gone, that part of us went with him, our home is so empty now without him, our only consolation is that Charlie had a wonderful life while he was with us. We made his life worth living. He came from a living hell to having a life worth living, a life full of love and happiness. He was a joy to be with and gave joy to others, when he was around. He shall be sadly missed but will always be remembered, never forgotten.

Charlie was taken from us on the
2nd March 2021
He was aged around 12
When God took him he shall be
loved.
And never forgotten.
This book has been written in
dedication to his memory

Charlies resting place

Sympathy cards

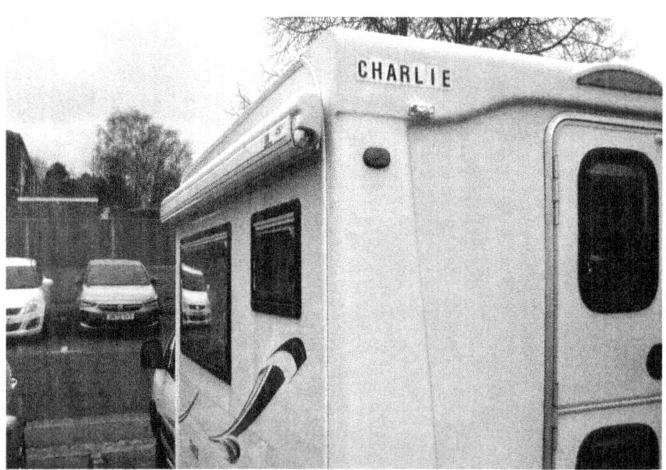

The camper van with Charlies name on it

Close up of the plaque on Charlies Gate

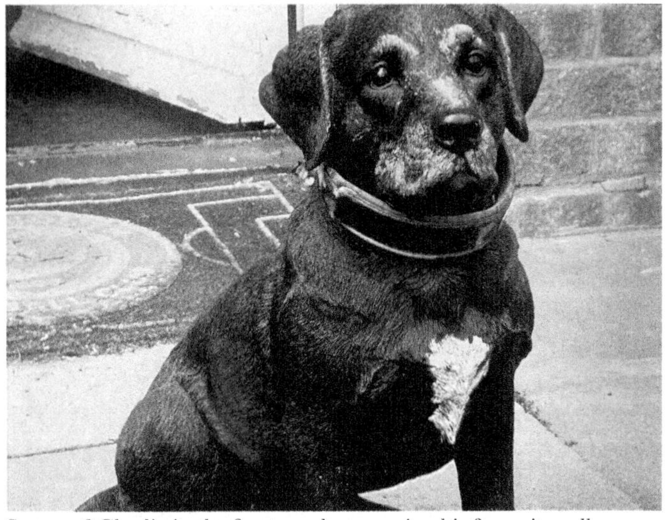
Statue of Charlie in the front garden, wearing his favourite collar

FOR THE LOVE OF CHARLIE

Printed in Great Britain
by Amazon

39290018R00056